26/GS Publications/1178

I0165175

SHOOT TO KILL

Part X.
Basic and battle physical training
1944

The Naval & Military Press Ltd

Published by

The Naval & Military Press Ltd
Unit 5 Riverside, Brambleside
Bellbrook Industrial Estate
Uckfield, East Sussex
TN22 1QQ England

Tel: +44 (0)1825 749494

www.naval-military-press.com
www.nmarchive.com

In reprinting in facsimile from the original, any imperfections are inevitably reproduced and the quality may fall short of modern type and cartographic standards.

Shoot to kill
Part X. Basic and battle physical training 1944

Prepared under the direction of the Chief of the Imperial General Staff.

THE WAR OFFICE　　　　　　　　　　　　AUGUST, 1944

RESTRICTED

The information given in this document is not to be communicated, either directly or indirectly, to the Press or to any person not authorized to receive it.

CROWN COPYRIGHT RESERVED.

Contents:
PAGE

Introduction 1

Standard One—Elementary
Exercise
1. GRIP (Alternate grip release) 4
2. DEXTERITY (Rifle change) 5
3. SHOULDER (Rifle pointing sideways) 6
4. WRIST (Under swing and check) 7

Standard One—Intermediate
5. GRIP (Alternate muzzle and butt lowering) 8
6. DEXTERITY (Grip reversing)... 9
7. SHOULDER (One-handed swing round head) 10
8. WRIST (Winding) 11

Standard One—Advanced
9. GRIP (Forward hip hold) 12
10. DEXTERITY (Hand to hand throw) 13
11. SHOULDER (Shoulder rolling) 14
12. WRIST (Outward circle) 15

Standard Two—Elementary
13. GRIP (Vertical raise) 16
14. DEXTERITY (Climbing up and down rifle) 17
15. SHOULDER (Circling sideways) 18
16. WRIST (Wrist turning) 19

Standard Two—Intermediate

Exercise	PAGE
17. GRIP (Single shoulder lift)	20
18. DEXTERITY (Aim and twist)	21
19. SHOULDER (Side circles)	22
20. WRIST (Shoulder circle one hand)	23

Standard Two—Advanced

21. GRIP (Wrist bending and stretching)	24
22. DEXTERITY (Front circling)	25
23. SHOULDER (Double forward-under circles)	26
24. WRIST (Under-overswings)	27

Standard Three—Elementary

25. GRIP (Forward lowering and raising muzzle)	28
26. DEXTERITY (Overtwist)	29
27. SHOULDER (High circles)	30
28. WRIST (Circling to kneeling position)	31

Standard Three—Intermediate

29. GRIP (Forward raising and lowering with both hands)	32
30. DEXTERITY (Vertical twist)	33
31. SHOULDER (Two-handed swing overhead)	34
32. WRIST (Kneeling, wrist rotating)	35

Standard Three—Advanced

33. GRIP (Aim in eight movements)	36
34. DEXTERITY (Side reach and change)	37
35. SHOULDER (Lying, alternate arm bending and stretching)	38
36. WRIST (Lying, twisting)	39

Distribution

1 per A.P.T.C. Instructor

Primary Training Centres	Scale B
Infantry Training Centres	Scale D (a)
Other Corps Training Units	Scale D (a)
O.C.T.U's	Scale III
All other Units	Scale B
Army School of Physical Training	600 copies
Command P.T. Schools	200 copies
Small Arms School (Hythe Wing)	50 copies
Small Arms School (Netheravon Wing)	20 copies
School of Infantry	20 copies
Advanced Handling and Fieldcraft School	20 copies

Physical training for weapon training

Introduction

1. OBJECT
Physical Training for Weapon Training has only one object—to enable the soldier to acquire complete mastery over his weapon so that he will use it skilfully and effectively in battle.

2. PRINCIPLES
Good shooting largely depends on the soldier's confidence in his rifle and an unshakeable belief in his own power and skill. He must hold his rifle in good respect and cultivate for it an understanding so complete that only he himself can appreciate its true merits. He must handle his rifle with equal facility by day and by night and when moving quickly or when moving stealthily. In short, he must be able to shoot with deadly effect in any position and under any circumstances.

The following exercises are designed to promote confidence by developing strength in the muscles of the shoulders, arms, wrists and hands, and by improving dexterity and skill in weapon handling.

In addition, quick reaction may be stimulated by using firing positions and fieldcraft movements from time to time, as brain stimulators during the practice of the exercises.

Rest position
(Astride, butt on ground, hands at outer band)

3. ARRANGEMENT OF EXERCISES
There are three Standards of exercises, with an Elementary, Intermediate and Advanced Part in each Standard. In each Part the exercises follow the same sequence, namely, Grip, Dexterity Shoulder and Wrist. Standard 1 should be carried out in Tables 4–6 of Corps Physical Training. Standards 2 and 3 are intended for Trained Soldiers to be used during Drill, Weapon Training, or Physical Training Periods.

4. APPLICATION
(a) The exercises can be included either in a Weapon Training or a Physical Training period. To be of maximum value the exercises should be performed at least once daily.

(b) Before carrying out the exercises, rifles should be inspected, targets indicated, actions cocked, safety catches applied and slings loosened.

(c) The instructor himself will set the exercises with his own rifle.

(d) To prevent injuries from swinging rifles, the class should be well spaced.

(e) Slings which are loose should be taken up in the hand during all swinging exercises.

(f) The Ready Position for all exercises is feet astride, arms downward and hands gripping the rifle, the right hand in overgrasp at the small of the butt and the left hand in undergrasp at the outer band. The thumb must be round the rifle in both overgrasp and undergrasp.

(g) To assume the Rest Position the butt is lowered to the ground, the hands grasping the rifle at the outer band.

(h) A complete Standard of exercises will take approximately 7 minutes to perform. This time will vary, however, according to the capabilities of the class, the stage of training and the number of times each exercise is repeated.

(i) In the early stages of training only one Part of a Standard should be taken in one lesson, each exercise being taught separately. If properly applied, one Part should not take more than $2\frac{1}{2}$ to 3 minutes to perform. Later, the exercises should be linked together, and the Part carried through without a pause. Finally, all three Parts should be linked together to form a complete Standard of exercises.

(j) One-handed or one-sided exercises should be repeated to both sides.

(*k*) The class must be kept alert by the frequent use of " quickeners " or brain stimulating activities. For this purpose firing positions may be used on a visual or auditory signal from the instructor. These quickeners must be unexpected and come as a surprise. They may be used at any time during the lesson.

(*l*) When taking up a firing position the safety catch should be pushed forward and the first pressure taken ; the safety catch being re-applied when the exercises are re-commenced (except Exercise 17).

(*m*) In the description of the exercises the Starting Position is always given in brackets.

Ready position for all exercises

Feet astride, arms downward, hands gripping the rifle, the right hand in overgrasp at the small of the butt and the left hand in undergrasp at the outer band. The thumb must be round the rifle in both overgrasp and undergrasp.

Standard One Elementary

Exercise 1

GRIP (Alternate grip release)

(Astride, arms downward, alternate grasp)

Releasing grip with each hand alternately.

Note:

1. *The hand must be turned outward (i.e. palm to front) clear of the rifle.*

2. *The position is held longer as strength is developed.*

DEXTERITY (Rifle change)

2

(Astride, arms downward, alternate grasp)

Releasing grip and swinging rifle to reverse position (i.e. muzzle travels from left to right).

Note:

1. *The position of the hands on the rifle is changed.*

2. *During the swing the rifle must pass from side to side, through the vertical position in front of the body.*

SHOULDER (Rifle pointing sideways)

3

(Astride, arms downward, alternate grasp)

Releasing left (right) hand grip and trunk turning with right (left) hand pointing rifle to left and left (right) arm swinging sideways-backward and opposite heel raising.

Note :

1. *The position is held longer as strength is developed.*

2. *Exercise should be repeated, pointing rifle to right.*

WRIST (Under swing and check) 4

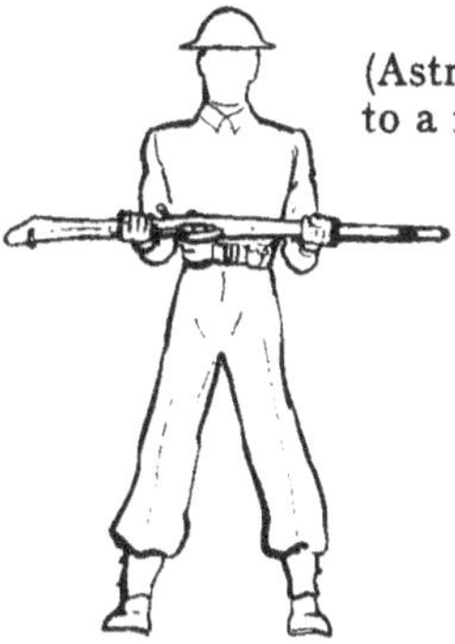

(Astride, arms forward, elbows bent to a right angle, under grasp)

Releasing left (right) hand grip and swinging rifle downward-sideways to right (left) and checking when rifle is parallel with ground with (left) right hand.

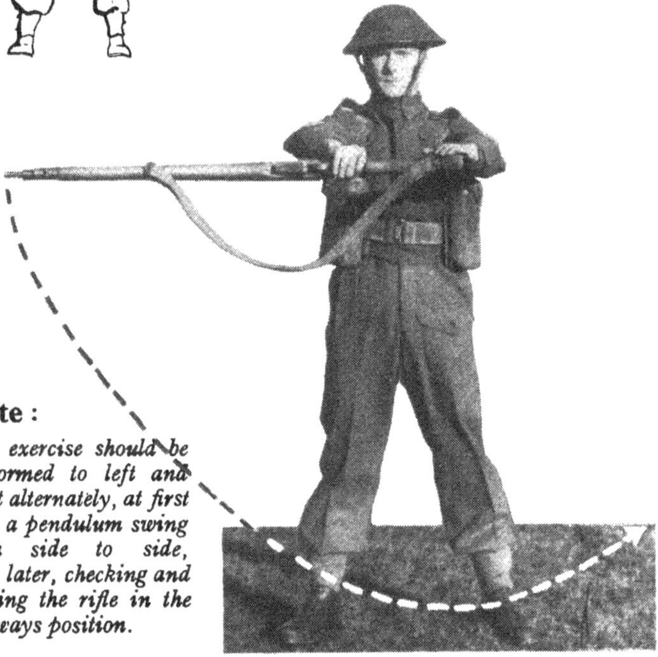

Note :
The exercise should be performed to left and right alternately, at first with a pendulum swing from side to side, and, later, checking and holding the rifle in the sideways position.

QUICKENER (Standing aim and later swinging at an air target)

See SMALL ARMS TRAINING, Vol. 1, Pamphlet No. 3, Rifle, 1942.

Standard One Intermediate

5

GRIP (Alternate muzzle and butt lowering)

(Astride, arms downward, alternate grasp)

Releasing left hand grip and lowering and raising muzzle, followed by releasing right hand grip and lowering and raising butt.

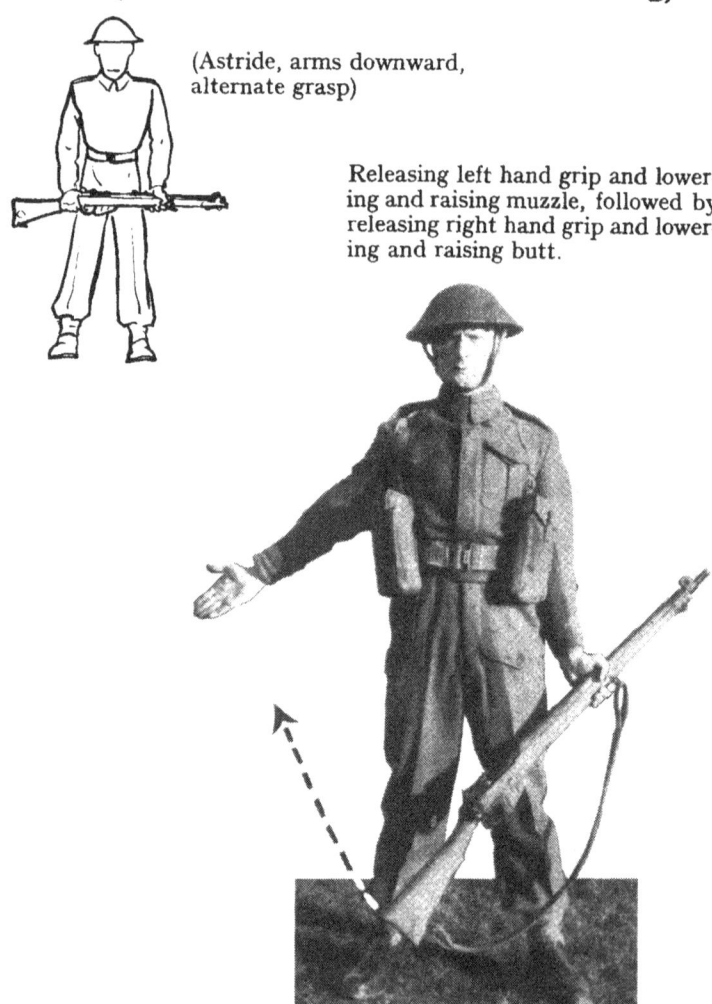

DEXTERITY (Grip reversing) 6

(Astride, arms forward, alternate grasp)

Reversing grip with each hand alternately.

Note :

With beginners the exercise should be done once only with each hand and then the arms lowered to the ready position for a short rest. After this the exercise should be again repeated. Gradually, as strength is developed, the grip should be reversed several times before the rifle is lowered.

SHOULDER (One-handed swing round head) 7

(Astride, arms downward, alternate grasp)

Releasing left hand grip, swinging rifle round head with right hand. Repeat with left hand.

Note :

1. *With beginners, the rifle should be raised in front of body and face with both hands before the grip is released. Later, as strength is developed, the hand grip should be released as soon as the exercise is begun.*

2. *The rifle must come to rest in both hands after each swing.*

WRIST (Winding)

8

(Astride, arms forward, overgrasp)

Twisting rifle alternately forward and backward in both hands.

QUICKENER (Kneeling aim in varying directions, using sound and visual targets)
See SMALL ARMS TRAINING, Vol. 1, Pamphlet No. 3, Rifle, 1942.

Standard One Advanced

9

GRIP (Forward hip hold)

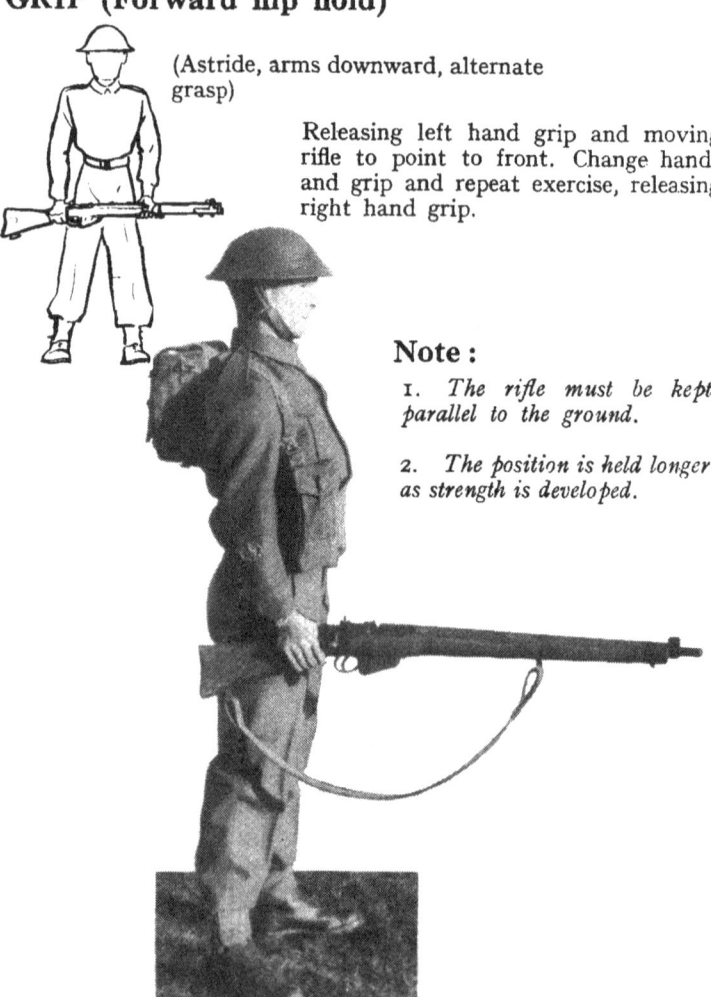

(Astride, arms downward, alternate grasp)

Releasing left hand grip and moving rifle to point to front. Change hands and grip and repeat exercise, releasing right hand grip.

Note:

1. *The rifle must be kept parallel to the ground.*

2. *The position is held longer as strength is developed.*

DEXTERITY (Hand to hand throw) 10

(Astride, right arm forward, elbow bent to a right angle, grasp at point of balance, rifle vertical)

Passing rifle from hand to hand.

Note:

1. *The distance between the hands should be increased as dexterity is developed.*

2. *This exercise may also be used as a quickener, the rifle being passed quickly from hand to hand a given number of times.*

SHOULDER (Shoulder rolling) 11

(Astride, rifle held in front of and close to chest, elbows to sides, overgrasp)

Alternate shoulder rolling forward and backward, large and small circles.

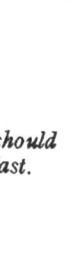

Note:
The speed of the exercise should be varied from slow to fast.

WRIST (Outward circle) 12

(Astride, arms forward, elbows bent to a right angle, undergrasp)

Releasing left hand grip, swinging rifle downward-sideways-over and catching at the outer band in the left hand. Change hands and repeat exercise, releasing right hand grip.

Note:

At the completion of the overswing movement the wrist will be twisted and it will be necessary to change the grip before commencing the next swing.

QUICKENER (Standing A A aim with footwork and movement)

See SMALL ARMS TRAINING, Vol. 1, Pamphlet No. 6, Anti-Aircraft.

Standard Two Elementary

13

GRIP (Vertical raise)

(Astride, arms forward, elbows bent to a right angle, alternate grasp)

Releasing left hand grip and raising rifle to the vertical and lowering to starting position with the right hand. Change hands and repeat exercise, releasing right hand grip.

DEXTERITY (Climbing up and down rifle) 14

(Astride, arms forward, holding rifle vertical with both hands on the butt)

Moving hand over hand (small movements) up and then down the rifle.

SHOULDER (Circling sideways) | 15

(Astride, arms downward, rifle grasped in right hand at point of balance)

Circling rifle upward-sideways-downward. Change hand and repeat exercise with left hand.

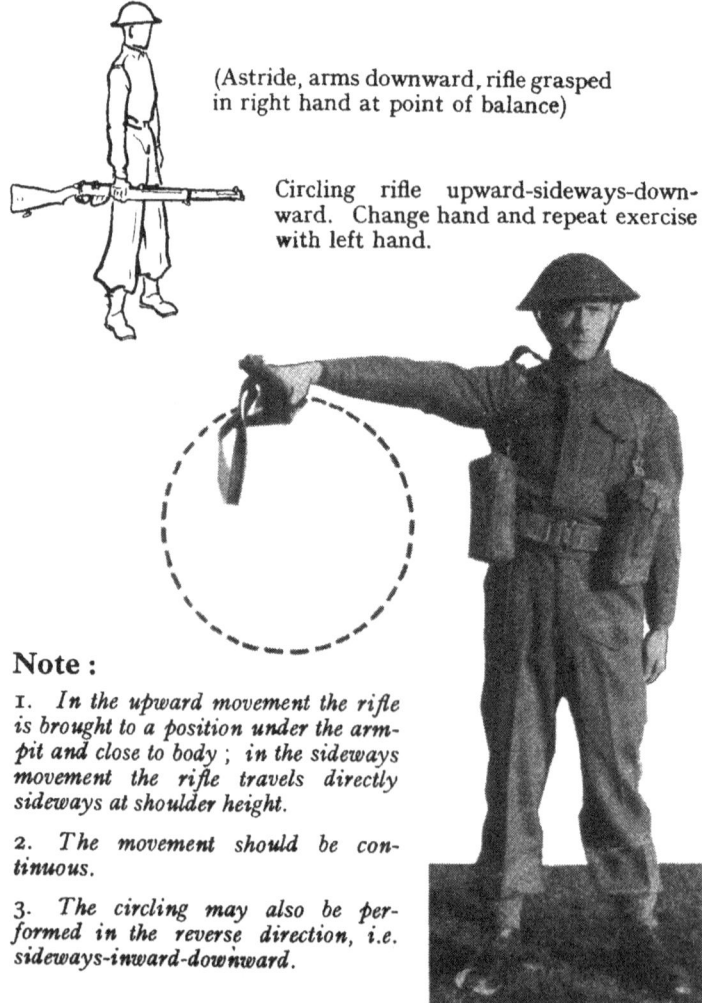

Note:

1. *In the upward movement the rifle is brought to a position under the armpit and close to body; in the sideways movement the rifle travels directly sideways at shoulder height.*

2. *The movement should be continuous.*

3. *The circling may also be performed in the reverse direction, i.e. sideways-inward-downward.*

WRIST (Wrist turning)

16

(Astride, right arm forward, elbow bent to a right angle, grasp at point of balance, rifle vertical)

Wrist turning upward and downward. Change hands and repeat exercise with left hand.

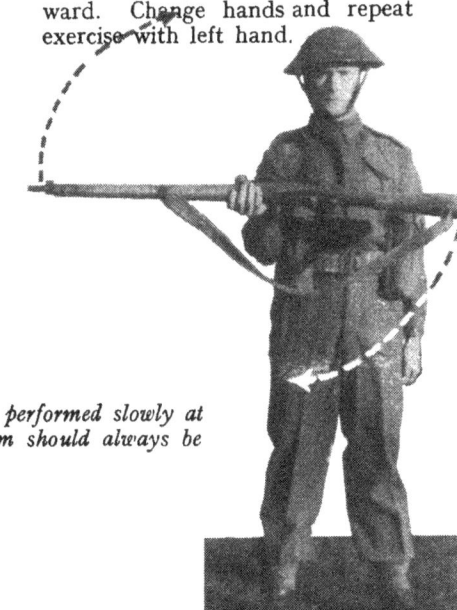

Note :

The exercise should be performed slowly at first and the upper arm should always be held close to the body.

QUICKENER (Walking, observing, freezing, and on signal, assume "On guard" position quickly and quietly)

Note :

1. *On the signal, change from " freezing " position to the " on guard " position.*

2. *The rifle is carried in the left hand at the point of balance and is held obliquely across the body.*

Walking—*See* INFANTRY TRAINING, Part VIII, 1944.

Standard Two Intermediate

17

GRIP (Single shoulder lift)

(Astride, arms downward, alternate grasp)

Releasing left hand grip, raising rifle to right shoulder with right hand. Change hands and repeat exercise, releasing right hand grip.

Notes:

1. The butt of the rifle must be pressed close to the shoulder as in the standing aim position and the elbow raised sideways in line with the shoulder.

2. The opposite arm is raised sideways to help in the maintenance of balance.

3. In the early stages of training men may find it difficult to raise the rifle with one hand only and some help may be necessary from the other hand.

DEXTERITY (Aim and twist) 18

(Standing aim)

Transferring right hand to point of balance and left hand to outer band and twisting the rifle backward through a complete circle,

followed immediately by twisting the rifle forward through a complete circle and resuming the standing aim position.

SHOULDER (Side circles) 19

(Astride, right arm sideways, palm turned upward grasping butt of rifle, left arm bent across the front of the body, grasping rifle at nosecap, with the left hand just below the chin)

Right arm circling backward and forward. Change hands and repeat exercise with left arm.

Note :

1. In the starting position the rifle should be supported along the outstretched arm.

2. To change hands the rifle is swung downward and sideways in front of the the body to the opposite side, the position of the hands on the rifle being reversed.

WRIST (Shoulder circle one hand) 20

(Standing aim)

Releasing left hand grip and with the right hand circling rifle downward-backward-over to standing aim position. Change hands and repeat with left hand.

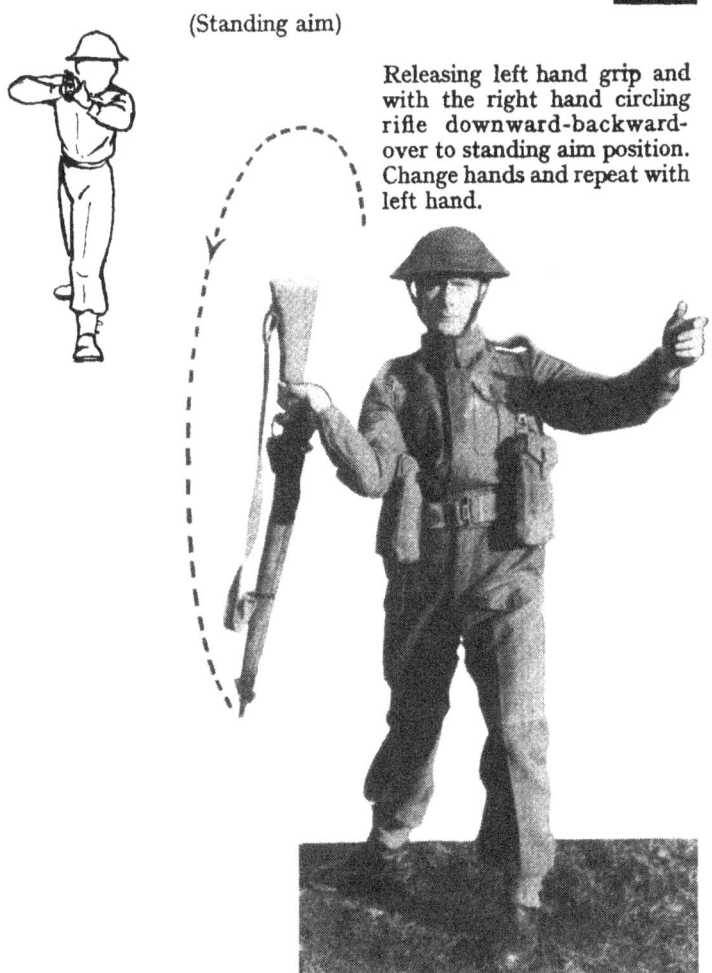

QUICKENER (Crouch running to kneeling aim)

Standard Two
Advanced

21

GRIP (Wrist bending and stretching)

(Astride, arms forward, overgrasp)

Wrist bending downward and stretching upward.

DEXTERITY (Front circling)

22

(Astride, right arm forward, elbow bent to a right angle, grasp at point of balance, rifle vertical)

Circling rifle outward (full circle) with the right hand. Change hands and repeat exercise with the left hand.

Note:

When the hand has rotated outward as far as possible it is necessary to grip the rifle with the other hand at a point near the back-sight. It is then possible to continue the circling movement with the right hand after changing grasp.

SHOULDER (Double forward-under circles) 23

(Astride, arms forward, overgrasp)

Circling the rifle in front of the body downward-upward-forward and inward-downward-upward.

Note :
The circling movements may be either small or large.

WRIST (Under-overswings)

24

(Astride, arms forward, undergrasp)

Releasing left hand grip, swinging muzzle of rifle downward-sideways-over and catching with the left hand just above outer band, followed by releasing right hand grip, swinging butt of rifle downward-sideways-over and catching with the right hand at the small of the butt.

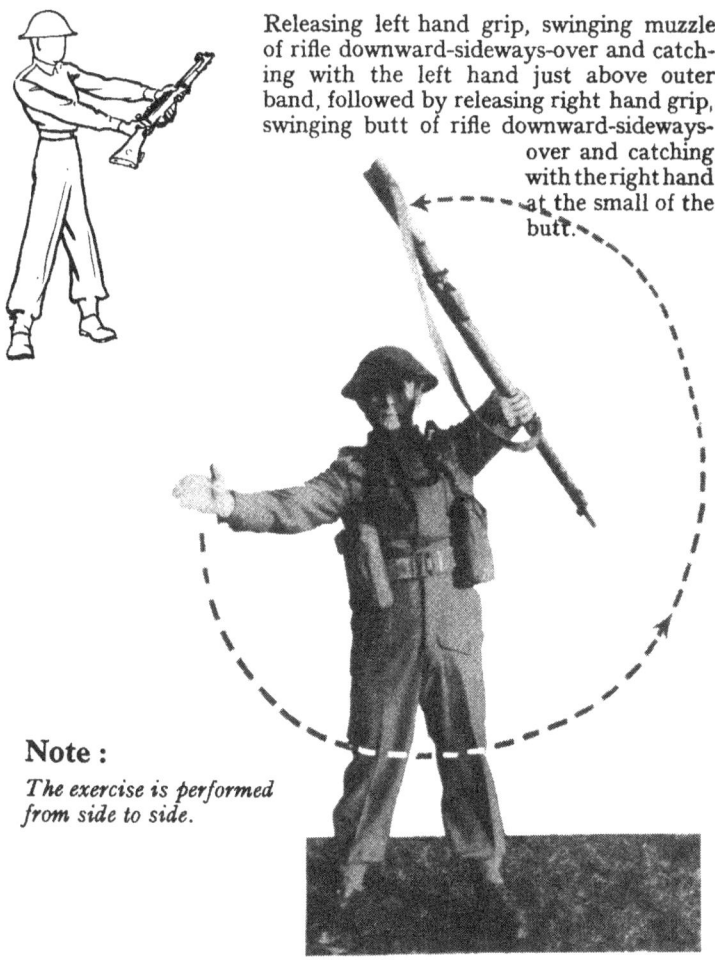

Note :
The exercise is performed from side to side.

QUICKENER (Walking, ground, tree or air target

Standard Three Elementary 25

GRIP (Forward lowering and raising muzzle)

(Astride, arms downward, alternate grasp)

Releasing left hand grip, slowly point rifle forward with the right hand, slowly lower muzzle to about 6 in. from the ground ; slowly raise the muzzle until it is horizontal to the ground and return to starting position. Change hands and repeat exercise with left hand, releasing right hand grip.

Note :
As strength is developed each position should be held longer.

DEXTERITY (Overtwist)

26

(Astride, arms downward, overgrasp)

Transferring the right hand to the point of balance and with this hand twisting the rifle through a full circle to reverse position. During the twisting movements the left hand is transferred to the small of the butt and the right hand to the outer band. Change hands and repeat exercise with left hand.

Note :

After the first twist the rifle will have the magazine upwards. The twisting movement, however, should be continued until the rifle comes to rest in the original starting position.

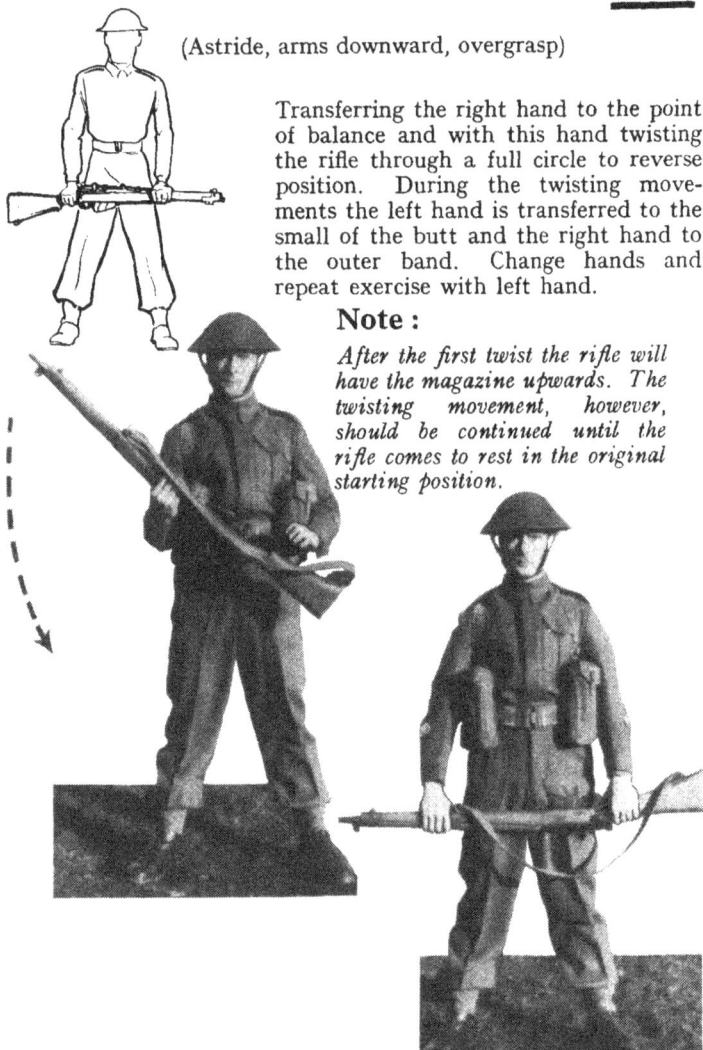

SHOULDER (High circles) 27

(Astride, arms upward, overgrasp)

Maintaining the grasp of the rifle with both hands, describe small or large circles forward or backward above the head.

WRIST (Circle to kneeling position) 28

(Astride, arms downward, alternate grasp)

Releasing left hand grip, circling rifle downward-backward-forward with right hand to catch at outer band with left hand. At the same time, advance the left foot and kneel on the right knee.

Change hands and repeat with left hand to kneeling position on the left knee.

Note :

The two movements—circling rifle and kneeling—should be timed so as to finish together.

QUICKENER. (Sitting aim, changing to lying aim facing rear and vice versa)

Standard Three Intermediate   29
GRIP (Forward raising and lowering with both hands)

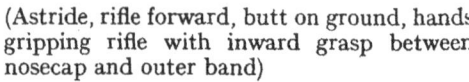

(Astride, rifle forward, butt on ground, hands gripping rifle with inward grasp between nosecap and outer band)

Raising rifle forward to shoulder height and lowering to starting position.

Note:

1. *The starting position is similar to the golf stance.*

2. *The upright position of the body must be maintained during the raising and lowering movements.*

3. *The movements must be performed slowly.*

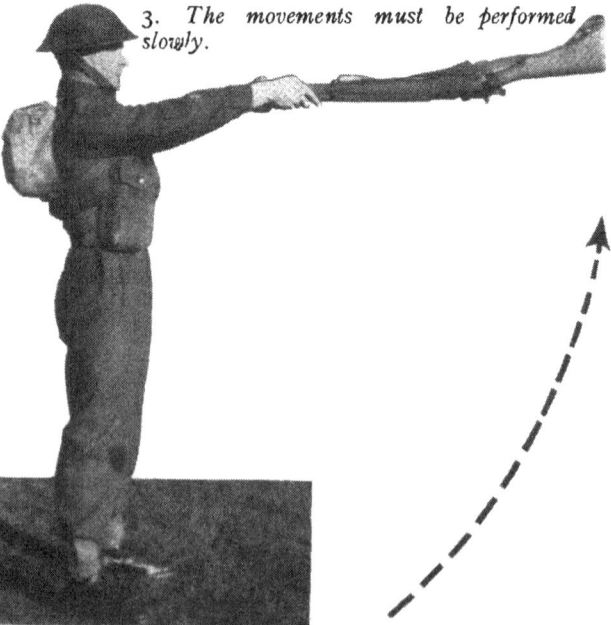

DEXTERITY (Vertical twist)

30

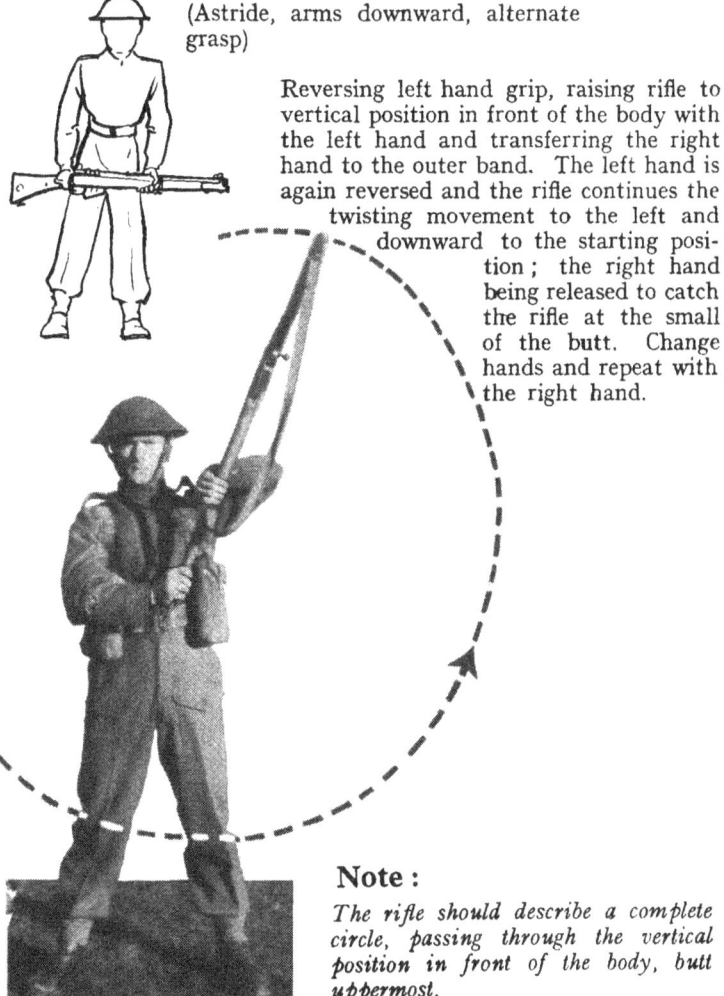

(Astride, arms downward, alternate grasp)

Reversing left hand grip, raising rifle to vertical position in front of the body with the left hand and transferring the right hand to the outer band. The left hand is again reversed and the rifle continues the twisting movement to the left and downward to the starting position; the right hand being released to catch the rifle at the small of the butt. Change hands and repeat with the right hand.

Note:

The rifle should describe a complete circle, passing through the vertical position in front of the body, butt uppermost.

SHOULDER (Two-handed swing over head) 31

(Astride, rifle forward, butt on ground, hands gripping rifle with inward grasp between nosecap and outer band)

Swinging rifle round the head with both hands, describing a complete circle to left and then to right.

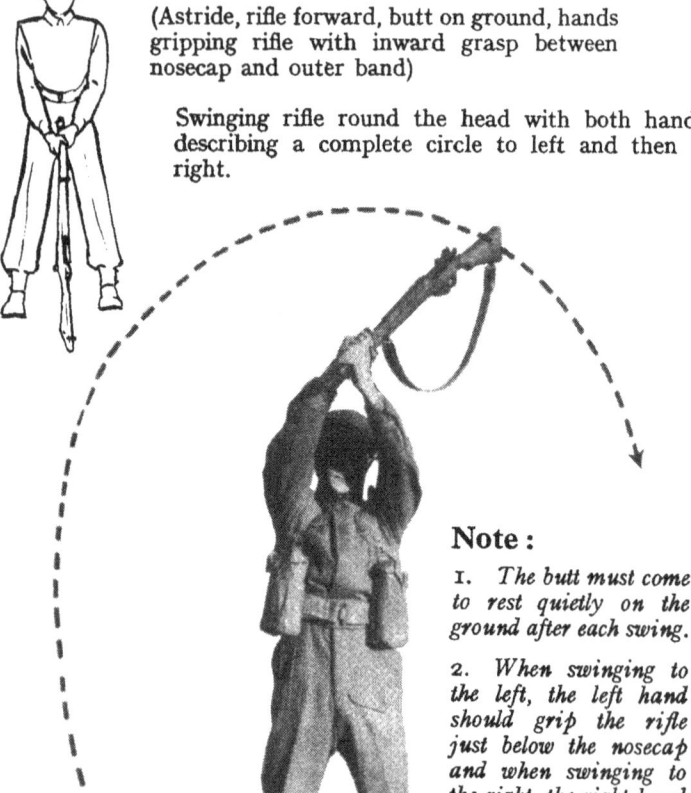

Note :

1. The butt must come to rest quietly on the ground after each swing.

2. When swinging to the left, the left hand should grip the rifle just below the nosecap and when swinging to the right, the right hand should grip just below the nosecap.

WRIST (Kneeling, wrist rotating) 32

(Kneeling on right knee, left hand gripping rifle at point of balance, left forearm on left knee, right hand on small of butt, rifle horizontal)

Striking small of butt with right hand, rotate the rifle muzzle to the right, and catching with the right hand at the outer band. To return the rifle to the starting position, strike it underneath with the right hand and rotate it in the reverse direction, catching it with the right hand at the small of the butt.

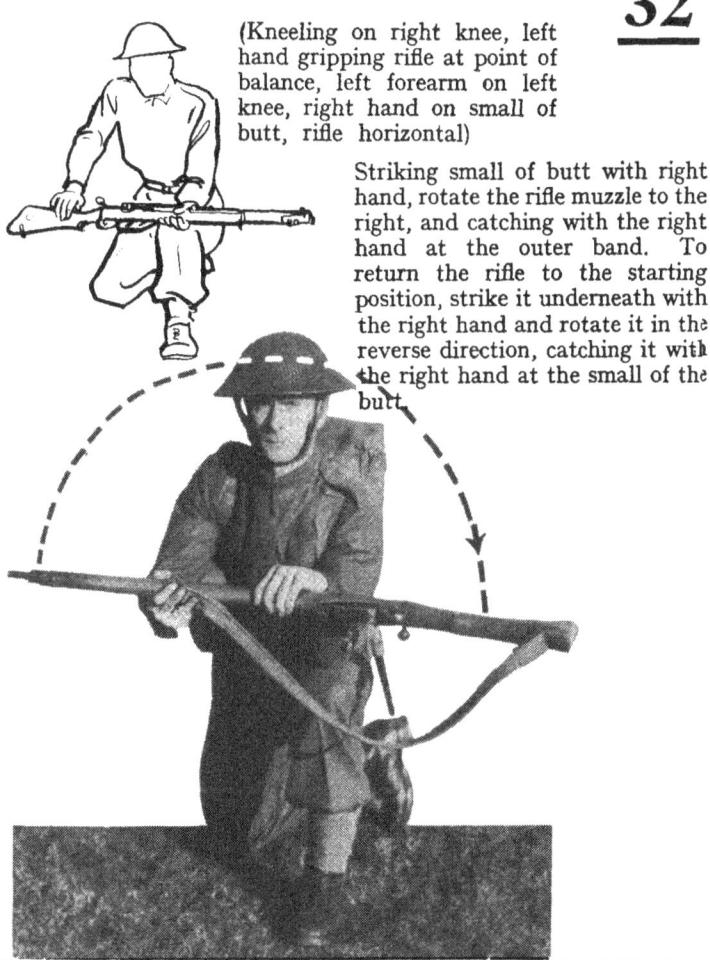

QUICKENER (Lying position changing to standing, sitting or kneeling position)

Standard Three Advanced

33

GRIP (Aim in eight movements)

Starting position for all the following is: (Astride, arms downward, alternate grasp)

(i) Releasing left hand grip, raise rifle to shoulder with right hand.
(ii) Advance left foot and place left hand at point of balance assuming standing aim position.
(iii) Release grip with right hand.
(iv) Return right hand to small of butt.
(v) Release grip with left hand.
(vi) Return left hand to point of balance.
(vii) Carry left foot backward to astride position and at the same time release grip with left hand.
(viii) Lower rifle with right hand to starting position.

Change hands and repeat exercise with left hand.

DEXTERITY (Side reach and change) 34

(Astride, arms downward, overgrasp)

Swinging rifle sideways to the right to shoulder height, changing grip with right hand and placing this hand at the point of balance; swinging the rifle downward-inward with the right hand and, at the same time, releasing left hand grip and changing this hand to the small of butt.

This is followed by changing the right hand grip to the outer band, which brings the rifle back to the starting position, except that the muzzle points in the opposite direction. Repeat the exercise, swinging the rifle to the left side and releasing left hand grip.

Note:

As strength and dexterity are developed, the exercise should be performed smoothly from side to side.

SHOULDER (Lying, alternate arm bending and stretching) — 35

(Lying, astride, heels down, rifle held at right side of body, right hand at small of butt, left hand at outer band)

Keeping rifle just clear of the ground, move it forward with both hands until the left arm is straight, then, keeping the left arm stationary, straighten the right arm until the rifle is held at full extent of both arms and just clear of the ground. Bend the left arm, keeping right arm stationary; then bend the right arm and straighten the left arm.

Repeat this movement several times and then return to starting position with the rifle at the right side.

WRIST (Lying, twisting) 36

(Lying, arms bent to right angles, elbows on ground, alternate grasp, rifle parallel to ground and level with the face)

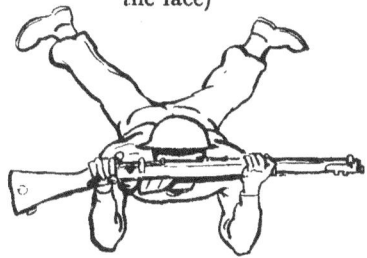

Twisting rifle forward and backward in both hands.

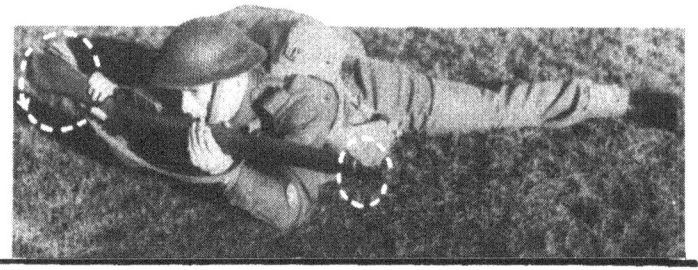

QUICKENER (Kneeling, followed by Leopard crawl and lying position)

Crawling.—*See* INFANTRY TRAINING, Part VIII, 1944, Section 3.

www.ingramcontent.com/pod-product-compliance
Lightning Source LLC
Chambersburg PA
CBHW022345040426
42449CB00006B/730